The Baking Evolution
Basic Recipes
For allergen-free living
By Kimberly Lay

Thank you to:

My parents for your sacrifice and support on this bumpy journey, and for always believing in me.

My Husband and children for being the driving force behind this book and forever changing my life.

Everyone who helped me along the way with tips, tricks, research, and taste testing.

Forward

By Mary Thompson

I was with Kimberly the day she first found out about Judah's food allergies. I was with her when she went from the doctor's office to the health food store and was not able to find one baked good he could eat. I saw her ready to break down into tears in the store, and then as we left gather up her strength to face the hard road ahead. Her father always told her "Can't never did anything". Obviously she took that to heart!

I watched Kimberly through her journey of baking discovery; her heartbreak, desperation, determination, triumphs, food disasters, and successes all the while being a devoted mom, wife and pursuing the challenges and joys of daily life.

It has been through her great faith, resolve, love for her children and with the support of her husband that the recipes in this cookbook have come into being. During this journey she has gained knowledge about healthy eating that has continued to amaze me. She also has developed a passion to share what she has learned with others. Not to mention that she can bake some delicious food!

The Baking Evolution made its debut at the Farmers Market this summer. I was her assistant. Every week exciting things happened. Customers loved her food! Many people on gluten free diets were amazed at the texture and flavor of her baked goods. She had repeat customers, and many came referred by friends who had tried her food. The double chocolate muffins were usually her biggest seller, but the strawberry scones, blueberry lemon bars and cookies were also best sellers.

Two encounters still touch me when I think about this summer. The first was a young boy who had food allergies. He was so excited after his mom read the label of ingredients and let him try samples. He was grinning from ear to ear! He came back and asked again, "Are you sure I can eat these? I'm not allergic?" They became regular customers. His mom told us it was so nice to be able to take him on an outing where he could have samples like his friends. Kimberly always made sure she had plenty of samples of his favorites!

The second encounter was a young woman. She had just been diagnosed earlier in the day with Celiac disease. She had come from the health food store and bought baked goods to try. She said they were terrible and so expensive. She tried samples of Kimberly's food, and started to cry. She remarked how good they were and she was so relieved to know she could find something that wasn't rubbery and tasteless. She thanked Kimberly for giving her hope to eat healthy and to be able to bake on her own. Kimberly talked to her a long time giving her baking advice and encouragement.

So many wanted recipes, and now the first cookbook is here! Although it might seem overwhelming at first, do not be discouraged you can do it! It will get easier as it goes, and the results are delicious! Remember: "Can't never did anything!"

Welcome to The Baking Evolution!

Do you have food allergies? Medical or religious/moral diet restrictions? In the pursuit of health and mental clarity? This baking company is dedicated to giving people wonderful alternatives for breads and desserts. If you are interested in alternative bread baking recipes and holiday recipes this book has something for you. I only publish recipes that have been tested repeatedly for taste, texture and reliability.

What makes my bread recipes different?

The inspiration for these recipes comes from my daily life. After my children were diagnosed with several food allergies, I searched endlessly to find recipes they could eat. After looking through thousands of recipes; I could not find a single bread recipe they could eat. Not only are my children on the gluten/casein/corn/soy free and low oxalate diet; they also are allergic to the substitutes used in GF/CF recipes. No potatoes. No tapioca. No sugar. No commercially processed yeast. I was determined that my children would eat bread and enjoy birthday cake. They would have muffins, cookies, crackers, and pies.

Realizing that I would have to create my own baking recipes, I took a scientific approach. I have broken down all of the ingredients in "regular" bread recipes to the basic chemical reactions that take place and substituted ingredients that together cause a similar reaction. I have studied and combined various techniques from contemporary, traditional and indigenous cultures to come up with the perfect bread recipes.

Table of Contents

Introduction...	11
Recommended equipment.............................	22
Preparations...	23
Daily Breads	27
Sorghum..	28
Multigrain..	29
Plantain Multigrain...............................	30
Flat/unleavened	31
Zucchini (unsweetened).....................	32
Plantain...	33
Pizza Crust..	34
Deep Dish Pizza Crust.........................	35
Focaccia	36
Native American Fry Bread................	37
Southern "Buttermilk" Biscuits.........	38
Biscuits..	39
Cakes	40
Chocolate with Chocolate Frosting.................	41
Lemon Pudding...	43
Carrot..	45
Banana Split...	47
Blueberry with Blueberry Frosting.................	49
Cantaloupe with Coconut Cream Icing............	51
Brownies...	53
Blondies..	54
Butternut Blondies..	55
Pumpkin Cream Roll..	56
Cranberry Jelly Roll...	58
Cookies	60
Chocolate Chip...................................	61
Lemon Drop..	62
Orange Spice......................................	63
Cranberry "Oatmeal".........................	64
"Sugar"..	65
Banana Cream....................................	66
Coconut Butter...................................	68
Molasses..	69
Muffins	70
Double Chocolate..	71
Blueberry..	72

	Banana..	73
	Spice..	74
	Pineapple Upside Down......................................	75
Breakfast	....	76
	Bagels..	77
	Pancakes...	78
	Banana Coconut Pancakes........................	79
	Honey Apple Spice Rolls............................	80
	Date Rolls...	81
Pies	....	82
	Crust #1 (best for pudding pies)...............	83
	Crust #2 (best for fruit pies).......................	84
	Custard...	85
	Chocolate Silk..	86
	Apple...	87
	Pumpkin...	88
	Date...	89
Scones	....	90
	Strawberry..	91
	Orange Cranberry...	92
	Lemon Berry..	93
	Pumpkin..	94
	Brown "Sugar" & Fig....................................	95

Introduction

This type of baking is very different than "normal" baking. Although at first glance the ingredients may not seem to go together; combined they create a chemical reaction that creates the desired result. It is extremely important to make proper preparations before baking. I usually set aside a time to just prepare the ingredient for the recipes before I plan to bake. At first this will seem like a lot of work, but once you get in the habit it will be easy. The first time I would recommend setting aside a half a day to thoroughly read through and prepare the ingredients. That being said, here is a note about cooking with each of the ingredients:

Rice Flour

The most important thing is to remember that you are still cooking with rice. Even though ground into flour, rice still cooks like rice. There is a period of soaking up all of the liquid followed by a period of internal steaming which creates the fluffy texture. Rice flour bruises easily during the mixing process. If you over mix your batter your finished product will be a gummy mess. Never use only one kind of rice flour in your baking; this will result in either a gummy product or a dry product. I recommend using a blend of rice that contains different textures to create a soft structure for your breads. The all purpose blend I use contains the following: long grain white, brown, arborio, jasmine, basmati or calirose. When I can find it, I use Jade Pearl, which is an exceptionally nutritional grain of rice.

It is more cost efficient to buy your rice in bulk and grind into flour yourself. Grinding your own rice flour also provides a healthier option because you can grind any variety of rice. The grinder I use is the Blendtec Kitchen Mill which can be found online or at Bed, Bath & Beyond. I like this grinder because it has different settings and grinds the flour very fine. If you do not wish to grind your own flour, you can purchase rice flour from your local grocer, health food store, or order online. Commonly the pre-ground flours come in white, brown, and sweet white.

Red Rice

Red, or pink rice is high in potassium, magnesium, vitamin B1 & B2, fiber, iron and calcium. This rice traditionally comes from India, Thailand, and Madagascar; however there is a new strain cultivated in the south of France. Red rice has a slightly sweet, nutty, and sometimes spicy flavor -similar to cinnamon, cloves, or nutmeg. (Lotus Foods, 2012, a) (Lotus Foods, 2012, c) (wikipedia, 2012, February 6) Red rice can be found at health food stores, Asian markets, or online.

Purple Rice

The following information comes from www.lotusfoods.com and www.en.wikipedia.org. Purple rice, also known as black or forbidden, is a sweet glutinous (meaning sticky and not to be confused with gluten). Purple rice is high in anthocyanins, a class of flavanoid antioxidants; contains a higher level of vitamins, minerals, fiber, protein, vegetable fat, and trace elements than other rice strains. Traditionally this rice comes from China and Thailand and was once reserved for royalty. Purple rice can be purchased from health food stores, Asian markets, or online. (Lotus Foods, 2012, b) (wikipedia, 2012, October 28)

Jade Pearl Rice

The Following information comes from www.lotusfoods.com. This rice is pearled rice with wild crafted bamboo extract added. Jade Pearl rice has a slight vanilla flavor and is full of chlorophyll. This rice can be found at health food stores and online. (Lotus Foods, 2012, d)

Arrowroot Starch

Arrowroot is a tropical herb; starch is extracted from the root stock. The starch is used as a thickener in cookies, jellies, breads, cakes, noodles, and sauces. Arrowroot is a purer starch than potato and can be ground into a smaller particle. This starch thickens at a lower temperature than corn starch and does not affect the color of sauces. Arrowroot is a pure carbohydrate and must be mixed with a flour containing protein for baking (wikipedia, 2012, November 12). Because arrowroot thins out with over cooking it makes an ideal ingredient in baking it thickens upon heating which helps add rise and structure to batters, then after prolonged heating, arrowroot breaks down and seems to disappear leaving desired air holes in bread. Arrowroot can be purchased at grocery stores, health food stores and online.

Xanthan gum

Xanthan gum is a polysaccharide derived from the bacterial coat found on plant sources. Xanthan gum is used as an emulsifier and thickener replacing gluten in baking and other cooking recipes. Some people may experience a similar reaction to xanthan gum and gluten; this does not seem to bother my family. If an allergic reaction is a concern, guar gum or locust bean gum can be substituted (Wikipedia, 2012, November 23). Xanthan gum can be purchased at most grocers, health food stores and online. Guar gum and locust gum can be purchased at health food stores and online.

Kudzu root starch

Kudzu or kuzu is a vine native to Asia. In baking kuzu is thickener and a binder. It is stronger than arrowroot, potato, and corn starches. Kuzu contains antioxidant properties, anti-inflammatory properties, and is a possible digestive aid for those with allergies. (wikipedia, 2012, November 30) Kuzu can be purchased at some health food stores, Asian Markets, or online. When purchasing kuzu make sure to find starch that has been ground up and crushed into small chunks with the fibers removed. Packages that contain whole kuzu root or large pieces will have fibrous material that is very difficult to remove.

Xylitol

Xylitol is an excellent replacement for white sugar; it looks like sugar and does not have a noticeable after taste. With a glycemic index of 6-7, xylitol is safe for diabetics and will not cause a sugar rush in children. It is used in toothpaste and will not cause tooth decay; in fact xylitol is thought to provide protection for teeth by helping to balance body pH and inhibiting the growth of bacteria. Xylitol is a sugar alcohol found in the fibers of fruits, vegetables, grains, and trees. Commercially xylitol is extracted from corncobs or birch trees. (wikipedia, 2012, December 4)

Some brands will specify the source; others may not and will then be a combination of sources. Corn based or mixed xylitol can be found at most health food stores and some grocers. The 100% birch based, or corn-free, type is harder to find but can be ordered online.

Palm sugar

Palm sugar comes in two forms: date palm sugar and coconut palm sugar. Date palm sugar is made from the sap of the date palm. Coconut palm sugar is made from the sap of cut flower buds. This type of sugar is an excellent low-glycemic replacement for brown sugar with an index of 35. Palm sugar is minimally refined so it retains its natural brown color, high mineral content and vitamins. (Wikipedia, 2012, December 1) Palm sugar can be found at health food stores and online.

Date syrup

This syrup is similar to molasses and is simply made from dates and water. You can purchase it from health food stores or make your own using the recipe in this book. Dates and date syrup are one of the original sweeteners of civilization dating back to ancient times (Date Lady, 2012). Dates are healthy and have a high mineral content. When mixed with palm sugar this is an excellent substitute for dark brown sugar. Date syrup may be used plain on pancakes, waffles and anything you would top with honey or syrup. Note: if you cannot find fresh dates, prunes may be substituted.

Kombucha

Kombucha is a fermented tea that has been around for thousands of years. This tea is extremely healthy containing numerous healthy acids, enzymes, beneficial bacteria, and local yeast (GetKombucha, 2012). This tea takes about 10 days to ferment and creates slow growing yeast that is beneficial for the gut. This yeast works great for people with digestive problems and does not have the strong taste or odor of sourdough. Although sugar is used to feed the culture and ferment the tea, no sugar remains at the end of the 10 day period. Kombucha works to balance and destroy Candida over growth; this ingredient creates safe yeast bread for people who suffer from yeast sensitivities. Bottled kombucha can be purchased at health food stores, but can be very expensive. A cheaper option is to grow your own, this is what I do. There are several websites that sell cultures and brewing supplies and offer free instructional videos. Because this is a 10 day process, I would recommend purchasing a few premade bottles so you can begin baking right away while waiting for your tea to ferment.

Coconut milk

I recommend using coconut milk in these recipes as a substitute for milk and buttermilk. If you have a coconut allergy any milk (rice, soy, seed, or nut) substitute can be used in a 1:1 ratio. I choose coconut milk for its medium chain fatty acids. As a mother of young children who must be milk free, I use coconut milk to provide healthy fats in their diet. While most people consume too much fat in their diet, they also consume the wrong kind of fat. Healthy fats are necessary for proper bodily functions (So Delicious, n.d.) . These fats also create a nice texture in breads. If you choose to use a different type of milk substitute, I highly recommend one that contains fatty acids. Milk alternatives are becoming more common and can be found at grocery stores and health food stores. Before purchasing read the ingredients, some brands contain additives and sugar.

Honey/agave/rice syrup

These syrups can be used interchangeably. In the recipes I recommend the syrup that I think works best for taste. Changing it out will not affect the texture, but the taste will change. In general agave syrup does not affect the taste of the finished product. Honey may not be suitable for diets.

Agar

Agar comes from algae on seaweed. It is used as a vegetarian gelatin used to make jellies, puddings, or custards. Agar contains up to 80% fiber and makes a healthy cooking agent aiding in intestinal regulation (Wikipedia, 2012, November 6). This can be purchased at Asian markets, health food stores, or online. When cooking with agar do not leave unattended, it will quickly boil over created a huge mess. Agar must be stirred frequently to ensure that the flakes melt and do not stick to the bottom of the pan.

Psyllium

Psyllium is a soluble fiber with many health benefits. It is the main ingredient in Metamucil. Psyllium relieves a variety of intestinal problems which makes it an excellent ingredient for people with food allergies. Pysllium also may help to lower and maintain blood sugar levels (University of Maryland Medical Center, 2011). In these recipes Pysllium is used as an egg replacer. It creates a gel like substance that provides structure and extra fiber. Pysllium can be found in whole flakes or powder at health food stores. If you prefer, you can use Metamucil.

Seed mixture

I use a seed mixture as another form of egg replacer; and to add nucleic acid and omegas to breads. Any of these seeds can be used alone, but I prefer to mix them together in equal parts to receive the most health benefit. The mixture contains: ground flax seed, chia seed, and hemp seed.

     Flax seed has been a very valuable food since ancient times. It contains high levels of Omega-3s, 1.8grams/tablespoon. Flax seed is one of the highest plant sources of lignans which contain estrogen and antioxidants. Flax is also a good source of soluble and insoluble fiber. (webMD, 2012)

     Chia seeds are also an ancient food source. They are higher in Omega3s and antioxidants than flax seeds. Chia seeds contain calcium, phosphorus, magnesium, manganese, copper, iron, molybdenum, niacin, and zinc (Weil, M.D., 2012). These seeds change texture in the stomach and slow down the process of breaking down carbohydrates (carbs). This changes simple carbs into complex carbs, helping to eliminate sugar highs/lows.

     Hemp seeds, first to be clear-hemp seeds are not marijuana, they will not get you "high" and you will not test positive on a drug test after eating them. Hemp seeds and other hemp food products are legal, usually imported from Canada, and can be purchased at health food stores and grocery stores like Hy-Vee. For verification of these facts go to www.TestPledge.com. Studies have shown that consumption of hemp seeds promotes learning, brain synapse activity, memory and immune function. Hemp seeds are a high source of vitamin E and fatty acids. (Kent, 2012)

Coconut flour

Coconut flour is a high fiber, high protein alternative flour. It has a wonderful taste that is slightly sweet. The coconut flavor is not strong and will not interfere with other flavors in baked goods. This flour can be purchased at health food stores and online. Because coconut flour has high oil content, it is not recommended to try and grind your own. Grinding it can clog the blades and break the motor. Coconut butter is created from adding coconut oil to coconut flour and mixing in a food processor.

Coconut butter

Coconut butter is a versatile ingredient; it can be used in place of peanut butter and cream cheese. Although some sources consider coconut to be a tree nut, it typically does not cause the same reaction. My children are allergic to peanuts and tree nuts, but have no reaction to coconut. If a substitution is necessary any seed butter can be used to replace coconut butter. Some health food stores carry hemp seed butter. Most grocery stores carry sesame seed butter, called Tahini. It is possible to make butter from pumpkin seeds and other similar squash. Coconut butter can be purchased in health food stores or online. It is possible to make it from coconut flakes, but it is hard to get a completely smooth consistency.

Beans

Many of these recipes call for bean paste. Typically I use a combination of green peas, yellow peas, red lentils, and brown lentils. Any mild flavor beans can be used; keep in mind that black beans will affect the color of your finished product. Red beans will not drastically affect the color but will show up as speckles.

Sorghum flour

Sorghum is a grass type grain that is ground into flour. Alone it does not provide adequate nutritional value, but it does add nice texture and flavor to breads. It cooks similar to corn meal or corn flour. Sorghum flour has a faintly sweet texture that can easily be drowned out by salt in a batter. For this reason always add at least one tablespoon of sweetener to sorghum bread recipes.

Spring roll rice wraps

These are cheap and easily found at Asian markets. The rice wraps help add texture and structure to bread recipes.

Recommended equipment

The following equipment is necessary to complete these recipes

1. Heavy duty food processor or blender
2. Ice cream scoop
3. Mixer
4. Glass tea pitcher or other acceptable container for kombucha
5. Large (2-4qt) well sealed container with lid.

The following equipment is recommended but optional

1. Grain mill, preferably one that has adjustable settings
2. Juicer

Preparations

All purpose rice flour

Remember it is essential to use a blend of different types of rice flour. In a large, 2-4 quart container mix the all purpose rice flour in the following ratio:

1c rice flour: 2T arrowroot: 1 tsp xanthan gum

I usually make 12 cups at a time so my ratio looks like this:

12c rice flour: 1 ½c arrowroot: ¼c xanthan gum

Place all ingredients in the container and shake well, about 3-5 minutes, until everything is thoroughly blended. Store the all purpose flour in this container for use. In addition to baking, this flour blend also makes excellent frying flour for poultry and fish or thickener for gravies.

Baking powder substitute (make this right before use)

1/2 tsp fresh lemon juice

1/4 tsp aluminum free baking soda

1/4 tsp kuzu

Add the lemon juice and kuzu to the liquid blend thoroughly.

Add baking soda to dry ingredients in recipes.

Bean paste

If mixing beans use even amounts. Soak beans in the following ratio:

1c beans (dry): 1T vinegar, lemon juice, or lime juice: 2c water

There are two methods of preparing the bean paste:

Method 1.

Place in pot on stove over low to medium/low heat. Soak in warm water until tender, but not thoroughly cooked. RINSE and process in food processor until ground into paste, will need to add small amount of water to form paste. The final paste should be thicker than soup but still moist. Each type of bean will need a different amount of water to reach this state depending on how long it was cooked. Store in a well sealed container and refrigerate.

Method 2.

Sprouting the beans, this method takes longer but may contain added health benefits and nutrients. Place ingredients in a bowl or jar and cover loosely. Daily rinse beans and change water until sprouted tail forms the same length as bean. Then rinse well and process in food processor until ground into paste, will need to add small amount of water to form paste. The final paste should be thicker than soup but still moist. Each type of bean will need a different amount of water to reach this state. Store in a well sealed container and refrigerate.

Fruit puree'

This is easily made in a food processor. For most recipes you will use apples which easily blend into the flavor of the finished product. I like to mix apples and peaches, because peaches are extremely sweet. Peel, core, and slice both apples and peaches, then chop in the food processor until smooth.

Any type of fruit can be used for specific flavors in recipes however other fruits will change the flavor and color of the finished product. An option for those of you who juice is to use the left over pulp from juicing; if you do this add 1-2 tablespoon of water to the recipe.

Date paste

Chop 10 dates, peel core and slice 2 apples or 1 apple and 1 peach. Chop in food processor until smooth and creamy. Option can substitute prunes if dates cannot be found.

Date syrup

1 lb fresh dates chopped, place equal parts dates and water into food processor and blend until completely smooth. Pour into a jar, cover and allow to sit for 24 hours before using.

***Option can substitute dates with prunes for equally good syrup.

Brown sugar substitute

1c palm sugar: 1 ½ T date syrup.

Mix together by hand until sugar is thoroughly coated with syrup.

Place in container or sealable baggie and store at room temperature.

Fruit molasses

4c fruit chopped in food processor

½c xylitol or palm sugar

1T lemon juice

Place all ingredients in sauce pan.

Cover and cook on medium heat until sugar is dissolved.

Reduce heat to low and cook for 70 minutes.

Place in jar and refrigerate.

Kombucha

Fermenting kombucha is a process that includes several steps, tips, and tricks. There are websites and books that provide supplies and instructions in great detail. Creating the perfect balance for your culture may take some time and practice, be patient.

Chapter 1
Daily Breads

*All bread recipes make 1 loaf or 4-5 rolls/buns unless otherwise specified.

Sorghum

Ingredients:

- 1 ½ c Sweet white Sorghum flour
- ½ c All purpose rice flour blend
- ½ c Sparkling Mineral Water
- ½ c Kombucha
- 1 c water or "milk"
- ½ tsp Salt
- ½ tsp Baking Soda
- 2 T Palm Shortening
- 1 T Sweetener

Instructions:

1. Place flours, salt, and soda in mixing bowl stir until well blended
2. Add shortening and sweetener, mix until "pebbles" form
3. Add liquids stir until blended in
4. Place in greased pan or tins, set oven to 350 and bake for 40-50 mins
   *This will be a batter not dough, it will set up like bread
   **DO NOT preheat oven. The bread will set up and rise as the oven is heating up. Placing the batter in a preheated oven will result in a gummy center.

Multi-grain

Ingredients:

- 1 c Sweet white Sorghum flour
- ½ c red rice flour (substitute any other grain flour, or just use sorghum)
- ½ c All purpose rice flour blend
- ½ c Sparkling Mineral Water
- ½ c Kombucha
- 1 ½ c water or "milk"
- ½ tsp Salt
- ½ tsp Baking Soda
- 1 T Palm Shortening
- 1 T Sweetener
- 1 T seeds (flax, chia, hemp, sesame, poppy)
- 1 T quinoa or millet
  *recommend using red quinoa (mild flavor) or roasted millet

Instructions:

1. Place flours, seeds, quinoa/millet, salt, and soda in mixing bowl stir until well blended
2. Add shortening and sweetener, mix until "pebbles" form
3. Add liquids until blended in
4. Place in greased pan or tins, set oven to 350 and bake for 40-50 mins
   *This will be a batter not dough, it will set up like bread
   **DO NOT preheat oven. The bread will set up and rise as the oven is heating up. Placing the batter in a preheated oven will result in a gummy center.

Plantain Multi-Grain

Ingredients:

- 4 rice spring roll wraps crunched up
- 1 banana or plantain mashed
- 1 1/2 tsp salt
- 1 1/2 tsp baking soda
- 2 T seed mixture
- 4T shortening
- 7T bean paste
- 1c hot water
- 1c water
- 1c kombucha
- 4c all purpose flour

Instructions:

1. In large mixing bowl add crunched rice wraps, seed mixture, banana or plantain, and 1c hot water. Mix until thoroughly blended and there are no chunks left.
2. Add in salt, baking soda.
3. Add bean paste and shortening.
4. Slowly mix in flour
5. Add 1c water and 1c kombucha.
6. Mix on high for 15 minutes.
7. Grease and lightly flour 1 large bread pan or 2 small bread pans.
8. Place batter in pan loosely cover and let sit for 6-8 hours.
9. Bake on 350 for 40 mins

Flat (unleavened)

Ingredients:

- 1 1/2tsp salt
- 1 1/2tsp baking soda
- 1Tblsp flax+3 Tblsp water
- 2 tsp raw honey or syrup
- 2Tblsp shortening
- 1Tblsp bean paste
- 2Tblsp oil
- 1/2c sparkling mineral water
- 1c "milk"
- 4c all purpose flour (multi-grain option: 1 1/3c all purpose + up to 2/3c red/purple rice blend)

Instructions:

1. Mix flax+water, salt, soda.
2. Add honey or syrup, shortening, oil
3. Add bean paste
4. Add "milk"
5. Slowly add flour and on high for 10 minutes or by hand for 15 minutes
6. Mix in sparkling mineral water
7. Scoop on to baking sheet or directly onto griddle and shape (ex. circles or squares)
8. Bake on 250 or fry on griddle

Zucchini (unsweetened)

Ingredients:

- 1 c Sweet white Sorghum flour
- ½ c All purpose rice flour blend
- ½ c coconut flour (substitute sorghum)
- ½ c Sparkling Mineral Water
- ½ c kombucha
- ½ c water or milk
- ½ tsp Salt
- ½ tsp Baking Soda
- ½ c shredded zucchini
- 1 T Sweetener

Instructions:

1. Place flours, salt, and soda in mixing bowl stir until well blended
2. Add zucchini and sweetener, mix until "pebbles" form
3. Add liquids until blended in
4. Place in greased pan or tins, set oven to 350 and bake for 40-50 mins
   *This will be a batter not dough, it will set up like bread
   **DO NOT preheat oven. The bread will set up and rise as the oven is heating up. Placing the batter in a preheated oven will result in a gummy center.

Plantain

Ingredients:

- 1 c Sweet white Sorghum flour
- 1 c All purpose rice flour blend
- ½ c Sparkling Mineral Water
- ½ c kombucha
- ½ c water or milk
- ½ tsp Salt
- ½ tsp Baking Soda
- ½ plantain sliced
- 1 T Sweetener

Instructions:

1. Place flours, salt, and soda in mixing bowl stir until well blended
2. Add plantain and sweetener, mix until "pebbles" form
3. Add liquids until blended in
4. Place in greased pan or tins, set oven to 350 and bake for 40-50 mins
   *This will be a batter not dough, it will set up like bread
   **DO NOT preheat oven. The bread will set up and rise as the oven is heating up. Placing the batter in a preheated oven will result in a gummy center.

Pizza Crust

Ingredients:

- 2/3c all purpose rice flour blend
- 1/3c coconut flour
- 1/3c sorghum flour
- 1/2c kombucha
- 1 c water
- 1/2c sparkling mineral water
- 1tsp salt
- 1tsp baking soda
- 2tsp pysllium flakes
- 1 T palm sugar
- 2T palm shortening

Instructions:

1. Place flours, salt, and soda in mixing bowl stir until well blended
2. Add shortening and palm sugar, mix until "pebbles" form
3. Add liquids until blended in
4. Spread out with a spatula on parchment paper
5. Top and bake on 400 for 15-20 minutes

Deep Dish Pizza Crust

Ingredients:
- 3c all purpose rice flour blend
- 4 rice spring roll wraps crunched (in food processor)+ 1c boiling water
- 1T flax
- 4T bean paste
- 1 tsp salt
- 1tsp baking soda
- 1c kombucha or sparkling mineral water
- 2T lemon or apple juice
- 1c water
- 2T oil

Instructions:
1. Mix salt, baking soda, flax, oil, and spring roll wraps+ water together.
2. Add bean paste and water
3. Add flour, mix on high for 10 mins
4. Slowly add kombucha or sparkling water and lemon juice
5. Shape dough into a ball and then spread over greased pizza tin or floured baking stone leaving a ridge to hold toppings
6. Top and bake 425 for 20-25 minutes

Focaccia

Ingredients:

- 2c all purpose rice flour
- 4 spring roll wraps + 1cup boiling water
- 4T bean paste
- 1/2 c "milk"
- 1/2 c kombucha or sparkling mineral water
- 1/4 c chilled shortening
- 1T xylitol
- 1tsp sea salt
- 1tsp baking soda
- 4T apple puree
- 1 cup herbs and veggies

Instructions:

1. Crunch up rice wraps in food processor and boil water. Mix together in a large mixing bowl
2. Cream together shortening, xylitol, salt, baking soda, apple puree. Add to rice wrap mixture
3. Add bean paste
4. Add liquid "milk" and kombucha or mineral water
5. Slowly add flour
6. Add herb and veggies*
7. Spread into a disk 1 1/2 in thick on greased baking sheet or floured stone. Cut into triangles or squares
8. heat oven to 400 and cook for 35 mins or until knife comes out clean

*at this point you may need to add more flour to get the consistency that you like. I suggest adding a 1/4c at a time until the batter starts to pull away from the sides of the bowl. For a more crumbly texture add more flour until batter forms into a ball.

Native American Fry Bread Makes 4 servings

Ingredients:

- 2/3c all purpose rice flour
- 1/3c sorghum flour
- 2T arrowroot
- 1tsp xanthan gum
- ½ tsp salt
- ½ tsp baking soda
- ½ tsp kuzu root
- 1 tsp coconut or rice flour
- ½ c water
- Vegetable oil for frying
- Extra sorghum flour (approx. 1c)

*for dinner top with meat and beans, for dessert top with honey or agave, spices, and fruit

Instructions:

1. In mixing bowl, blend 1c of sorghum flour, coconut or rice flour, arrowroot, xanthan, salt, baking soda
2. In a small bowl dissolve kuzu into water, then lightly blend into the dry mixture, do not over mix
3. Place extra sorghum flour in another bowl
4. With an ice-cream scoop or large spoon, scoop batter and drop it into the flour. Cover the batter completely with flour so that the outside is completely floured but the inside is sticky and has no extra flour (it is easier to pour the flour on top of the scoop of batter instead of trying to roll the batter in the flour)
5. Place oil 1" deep in a heavy pot, on medium heat, preheat to 350
6. With a fork, gently remove the ball of batter from the flour
7. Gently pat the ball flat until it is roughly 4"-5" in diameter
8. Gently drop dough into the preheated oil, fry for roughly 3 mins or until brown and then flip with tongs to finish other side (roughly 1 min)
9. Remove bread and place on paper towel. Can be kept warm in 200 degree oven for 1 hour or refrigerate and reheat at 350 for 10 mins

Southern "Buttermilk" Biscuits

By Jalisia Lay

Makes 9

Ingredients:

- 4c all purpose rice flour blend
- 2tsp salt
- 2tsp aluminum-free baking soda
- 2tsp kuzu
- 12T Earth Balance natural shortening, very cold
- 2T apple cider vinegar
- 2c coconut milk

Instructions:

1. Pre-heat oven to 375
2. In a large mixing bowl blend all dry ingredients except kuzu
3. Cut shortening into cubes, add to bowl, and cut into flour until it resembles coarse meal
4. In a separate bowl mix coconut milk, apple cider vinegar, and kuzu
5. Pour liquid into dry ingredients and mix with hands until just combined. Do not over mix.
6. Grease a 9x9 pan and pour dough in lightly spreading evenly
7. Bake for 20 mins

Biscuits

Ingredients:

- 1 1/2tsp salt
- 1 1/2tsp soda
- 1T flax+3 T water
- 2 tsp raw honey or syrup
- 3T shortening
- 3T oil
- 1/2c kombucha or sparkling mineral water
- 1c "milk"
- 4c all purpose flour (multi-grain option: 1 2/3c all purpose + 1/3c red /or purple rice blend)

Instructions:

1. Mix flax+water, salt, soda.
2. Add honey or syrup, shortening, oil
3. Add "milk"
4. Slowly add flour and on high for 10 minutes or by hand for 15 minutes
5. Mix in kombucha or sparkling mineral water
6. Bake on 300 for 15-20 minutes makes 12 2 inch biscuits

Chapter 2
Cakes

Chocolate with Chocolate Frosting

Ingredients:

Cake

- 1 1/3c all purpose flour
- 4T shortening
- 4T oil
- 1tsp salt
- 1 1/2tsp soda
- 1c xylitol
- 4T bean paste
- 4T apple paste
- 3/4c coco powder
- 2tsp vanilla
- 1/2c milk
- 1/2c water
- 1/2c sparkling water, or kombucha
- 2T apple cider vinegar or lemon juice

Instructions:

Cake

1. Cream together shortening, oil, salt, soda, xylitol
2. Add bean paste and apple paste
3. Slowly stir in coco powder
4. Add vanilla
5. Add all liquids
6. Slowly add flour and stir well
7. Grease and flour cake pan, pour in batter and bake at 350 for 25 minutes

Chocolate Frosting

- 1 can whole coconut milk
- 1c xylitol
- 3T agar
- ½ c arrowroot + ½ c coconut milk
- 4 squares unsweetened baking chocolate
- ¼c Rice syrup
- ¼ tsp vegetable glycerin

Instructions:

1. In a large sauce pan cook 1 can of coconut milk, 3T agar over medium heat, stir frequently. Bring to a boil and then simmer for 10 mins or until all agar flakes are dissolved.
2. Add xylitol and bring to boil again over medium heat. Still stirring frequently.
3. In a small bowl mix arrowroot and ½ c coconut milk. Add to the boiling mixture and continue to stir until the mixture becomes thick and bubbly.
4. Remove from heat and pour into a heat safe glass bowl.
5. Once mixture is cooled, in a double boiler melt chocolate and rice syrup.
6. Place all ingredients into mixing bowl and whisk until smooth and creamy. Add in glycerin and whisk 30 secs.
7. Frost cake when cooled

Lemon Pudding

Ingredients:

Cake

- 2 c all purpose rice flour blend
- ½ c xylitol
- 1tsp salt
- 1tsp baking soda
- ½ c palm shortening
- 1T apple cider vinegar
- ¾ c coconut milk
- 1 banana, sliced
- 8T lemon juice
- 4T coconut butter

Pudding

- 2c apple juice
- 3T agar flakes
- Dash of turmeric and salt
- ¾ c rice syrup
- ½ c agave
- ¾ c lemon juice
- ½ c arrow root
- ½ c coconut milk
- 1T lemon extract

Instructions:

Cake

1. Preheat oven to 350
2. In a small bowl or cup mix coconut milk with apple cider vinegar and set aside (this mixture will look like it is curdling, just let it sit)
3. In a large mixing bowl, blend flour, xylitol, salt, and baking soda.
4. Add shortening, sliced banana, and coconut butter mix until blended into coarse crumbs.
5. Add coconut milk mixture and lemon juice, stir until just mixed do not over stir,
6. the cake will be dense and tough
7. Grease and flour cake pan, pour batter in and spread evenly.
1. Bake for 25-30mins or until golden brown and pulled away from sides

Lemon Pudding

1. While cake is in oven begin pudding
2. In a small bowl mix arrowroot and coconut milk, set aside
3. Place apple juice, agar, turmeric, and salt in a large pot. Bring to a boil over medium heat. Reduce and simmer for 10 mins stirring constantly.
4. Add lemon juice, agave, and rice syrup, raise heat to medium. As soon as the mixture begins to boil whisk in arrowroot and coconut milk.
5. When liquid is thick and bubbly remove from heat and cool in pot for 10 mins.
6. Meanwhile with a toothpick gently poke holes in the top of the cake
7. Pour the pudding on top of the cake and allow to sit for 15 mins before refrigerating.

Carrot

Ingredients:

- 2c grated carrots
- 2/3c (fresh) or 8oz (canned) crushed pineapple, drained
- 3T pysllium+ ¾c water
- 1c shredded coconut
- 4T palm shortening
- 1tsp salt
- 1tsp baking soda
- 1tsp pie spice or allspice
- 1tsp vanilla extract
- 1 c xylitol
- ½c palm sugar
- 3c all purpose rice flour
- 2/3c sparkling mineral water
- 1/3c kombucha

Instructions:

1. In a small bowl mix pysllium+water and set aside.
2. In a large mixing bowl, mix carrots, pineapple, oil, shortening, coconut, and pysllium.
3. In a small cup mix salt, kuzu, lemon juice, vanilla, and baking soda. Stir into large mixing bowl.
4. Add xylitol and palm sugar
5. Add flour
6. Add sparkling mineral water and kombucha mix on high until blended and fluffy.
7. Evenly spread batter in a cake pan and bake on 350 for 45 minutes. Do not preheat oven.

Frosting:

Ingredients:

- 1c coconut butter
- 1 can whole coconut milk
- 1c xylitol
- 3T agar
- ½ c arrowroot + ½ c coconut milk
- ¼ tsp vegetable glycerin
- 2T vanilla extract

Instructions:

1. In a large sauce pan cook 1 can of coconut milk, 3T agar, and vanilla over medium heat, stir frequently. Bring to a boil and then simmer for 10 mins or until all agar flakes dissolve.
2. Add xylitol & coconut butter bring to boil again over medium heat. Still stirring frequently.
3. In a small bowl mix arrowroot and ½ c coconut milk. Add to the boiling mixture and continue to stir until the mixture becomes thick and bubbly.
4. Remove from heat and pour into a heat safe glass bowl.
5. Place all ingredients into mixing bowl and whisk until smooth and creamy. Add in glycerin and whisk 30 secs.
6. Frost cake when cooled

Banana Split

Ingredients:

Cake

Ingredients:
- 2 c all purpose rice flour blend
- ½ c xylitol
- 1tsp salt
- 1tsp baking soda
- ½ c palm shortening
- 1T apple cider vinegar
- ¾ c coconut milk
- 1c fresh crushed pineapple, plus juice
- 4T coconut butter

Instructions:
1. Preheat oven to 350
2. In a small bowl or cup mix coconut milk with apple cider vinegar and set aside (this mixture will look like it is curdling, just let it sit)
3. In a large mixing bowl, blend flour, xylitol, salt, and baking soda.
4. Add shortening and coconut butter mix until blended into coarse crumbs.
5. Add coconut milk mixture and pineapple/ juice, stir until just mixed do not over stir, the cake will be dense and tough
6. Grease and flour cake pan, pour batter in and spread evenly.
7. Bake for 25-30mins or until golden brown and pulled away from sides

Banana Pudding

Ingredients:

- 2 ¾ c whole coconut milk
- 3T agar flakes
- ¾ c agave
- ½ c xylitol
- ½ c rice milk
- 1/4c arrowroot
- 2 tsp vanilla
- Pinch of salt
- 2-3 bananas sliced

Instructions:

1. In a small bowl, mix rice milk and arrowroot.
2. In large sauce pan add 2c coconut milk, agar and salt. Stirring occasionally bring to boil over medium heat. Lower to simmer for 5-10 mins.
3. Add agave, xylitol and 3/4c coconut milk raise heat to medium.
4. When liquid begins to boil whisk in rice milk and arrowroot. Stir constantly until mixture is thick and bubbly
5. Remove from heat and allow to cool in the pot 15 mins
6. Meanwhile spread banana slices on top of cake, pour cooled custard evenly over cake

Glaze

- 1 cup strawberries (chopped) or cherries
- ¾ c+2 T apple or cherry juice
- 2tsp agar
- 1T agave
- 1T arrowroot

1. In a medium pan add ¾ c juice, fruit, agar, and agave. Bring to a boil over medium heat.
2. Mix 2T of juice and arrowroot together and whisk into boiling glaze.
3. As soon as the glaze begins to bubble remove from heat and drizzle over cake.
4. Allow to cool, place in refrigerator to finish setting up.

Blueberry with Blueberry Frosting

Ingredients:

Cake

- 3c all purpose rice flour blend
- 1tsp salt
- 1tsp baking soda
- 1tsp glycerin
- 4T bean paste
- 1c blueberry puree'
- 1c pomegranate juice (or other red juice)
- 1/2c kombucha
- 1/2c sparkling mineral water
- 1c xylitol
- 4T palm shortening

Frosting

- 2c xylitol
- 1c blueberry puree'
- 1c pomegranate juice (or other red juice)
- 1tsp vanilla
- 4T agar flakes
- 8T shortening
- ½ c coconut butter
- 1tsp baking soda
- 2T arrow root
- 1/4c coconut milk

Instructions:

Cake

1. In a large mixing bowl, mix salt, soda.
2. Add shortening, bean paste.
3. Add xylitol and cream together.
4. Add glycerin
5. Add blueberry puree' and juice
6. Slowly stir in flour
7. Stir in kombucha and sparkling mineral water
8. Grease and flour cake pan. Do Not preheat oven, cake will rise while oven heats up.
9. Bake one 350 degrees for 40-50 mins

Frosting

1. Mix agar, xylitol, blueberry puree', and juice in pan and bring to boil over medium heat. Once boiling lower heat and simmer for 10 mins. Immediately remove from heat and pour through a mesh strainer into a large mixing bowl.
2. Add shortening and mix on low.
3. Stir in coconut butter and mix until melted.
4. Add vanilla, glycerin, and soda.
5. In a separate bowl, mix coconut milk and arrowroot until smooth. Slowly pour mixture into large mixing bowl.
6. Whip on high until fluffy and creamy.
7. Refrigerate

Cantaloupe with Coconut Cream Icing

Ingredients:

Cake

- 4 rice spring roll wraps crunched up in food processor
- 1 tsp salt
- 1 tsp baking soda
- 1tsp kuzu
- 2 T physillium+4 T water
- 4T shortening
- 7T bean paste
- 1c hot water
- ½ c kombucha
- ½ c sparkling mineral water
- 2c cantaloupe puree'
- 3c all purpose rice flour blend

Icing

- 2c xylitol
- 2c coconut milk
- 7oz condensed coconut cream or coconut butter
- 2tsp glycerin
- 8T palm shortening
- 1T arrow root + 1/4c coconut milk

Instructions:

Cake

1. In large mixing bowl add crunched rice wraps, physillium, and 1c hot water. Mix until thoroughly blended and there are no chunks left.
2. Add in salt, baking soda.
3. In a separate bowl, mix kuzu with 4T water and add in
4. Add bean paste and shortening.
5. Add cantaloupe.
6. Slowly mix in flour
7. Add kombucha and mineral water.
8. Whisk on high until well blended.
9. Grease and lightly flour a bunt pan
10. Place batter in pan place pan in oven before turning on DO NOT preheat, cake will rise as oven heats up.
11. Bake on 350 for 40-50 mins.

Icing

1. In a medium sauce pan bring xylitol and coconut milk to a slow boil. Stir until xylitol is melted.
2. Stir in glycerine.
3. Stir in palm shortening.
4. Add condensed coconut cream (coconut butter)
5. In a separate bowl or cup stir arrowroot and remaining coconut milk together. Add to the pan and quickly whisk in. Continue to stir over heat until sauce becomes smooth and creamy.
6. Place in refrigerator and chill for at least 1 hr or until thick. Take out and whip in mixer or blender until fluffy. Then frost over cake.

Brownies

Ingredients:

- 4 squares of unsweetened baking chocolate
- ½ c oil
- 4T agave
- 4T apple paste
- 1/2c black beans cooked
- 1tsp salt
- 1tsp baking soda
- 1 1/2c all purpose flour
- 1c "milk"
- 1/2c sparkling mineral water
- 1c xylitol

Instructions:

1. In a double boiler melt chocolate squares and oil.
2. In large food processor, mix sweetener, agave, apple paste, black beans, salt, baking soda.
3. Once chocolate and oil are liquefied pour into food processor.
4. Add flour, water, and milk process until completely smooth.
5. Oil and flour a baking pan and place batter in pan.
6. Bake on 325 for 40 minutes

Blondies

Ingredients:

- 4 T coconut butter or coconut flour
- 1/2c oil
- 1/2c xylitol
- 4T raw honey or agave
- 2T apple paste
- 2T bean paste
- 1tsp salt
- 1tsp baking soda
- 1/2tsp glycerin
- 2c all purpose rice flour blend
- 1c "milk"
- ½ c kombucha or mineral water

Instructions:

1. Preheat oven to 325
2. In double boiler melt coconut butter and oil
3. In large mixing bowl, mix xylitol, raw honey/agave, apple paste, bean paste, salt, baking soda
4. Once coconut butter and oil are liquefied pour into mixing bowl and blend well.
5. Add glycerin
6. Add flour
7. Add milk and kombucha/mineral water
8. Mix on medium high for 5 mins
9. Oil and flour a baking pan and place batter in pan
10. Bake on 325 for 40 minutes

Butternut Blondies

Ingredients:

- 2c steamed chopped butternut squash
- 1 ½ c cooked (still firm) white beans drained and rinsed
- ¾ c coconut or palm sugar
- 10 dates, chopped
- 1tsp salt
- 1tsp baking soda
- ¼ tsp allspice or pumpkin pie spice
- ¼ c maple flavored agave
- ¼ c all purpose rice flour
- 2T coconut flour

Instructions:

1. Preheat oven to 350
2. Place all ingredients in food processor mix on high until completely smooth
3. Spread batter into a greased 8x8 pan, brownie pan, or dessert bar pan and bake 30-40 mins. Carefully check the bottom to make sure it is cooked all the way through even if a knife or toothpick comes out clean.

Pumpkin Roll

*Make cream filling before making cake. The filling will take a while to completely cool

Ingredients:

Cake

- ¾ c all-purpose rice four blend
- ½ c xylitol
- ½ c palm sugar
- 1tsp baking soda
- 2tsp spice (any of the following: pumpkin pie, allspice, ginger, cardamom)
- 1 c pumpkin puree'
- 1T bean paste
- 2T physillium (substation obtion: seed mix)
- 1tsp lemon juice
- 2T coconut flour+ 1T palm sugar for dusting

Instructions:

1. Preheat oven to 350
2. In a large mixing bowl blend flour, xylitol, palm sugar, baking soda, physillium/seeds, and spice
3. Add pumpkin puree', bean paste, and lemon juice
4. Grease and flour an 11x7 or 9x13 inch baking pan
5. Bake at 350 for 25-30 mins
6. Cut a sheet of parchment paper slightly larger than the pan and lay it on the counter.
7. Dust the parchment paper with coconut flour and palm sugar; carefully flip the cake onto the parchment paper.
8. Roll up the paper with the cake in it and allow to cool for 20 mins
9. Unroll the cake and spread filling on the inside. Immediately reroll the cake without the paper and wrap it in plastic. Store in the refrigerator.

Cream Filling

- 8oz coconut butter
- 1/4c shortening
- 1tsp vanilla
- 1c xylitol
- 1c water
- 1T kuzu+2T cold water

Instructions:

1. In a small sauce pan heat xylitol and water to make a simple syrup
2. Add coconut butter, shortening and vanilla. Continue to heat until bubbly
3. In a cup mix kuzu and water, whisk into bubbly sauce. Continue to stir constantly until well blended.
4. Remove from heat and pour sauce into heat safe bowl. Cool completely

Cranberry Jelly Roll

Ingredients:

- 3T pysllium+ ¾ c water
- 1c xylitol
- ¾ c all purpose rice flour
- 1/2 c sparkling mineral water
- ½ tsp salt
- ½ tsp baking soda
- 1 T kombucha
- ¾ c cranberry jam
- Extra xylitol for rolling

Instructions:

1. Preheat oven to 375
2. In a small bowl mix pysllium+3/4 c water and set aside
3. Line a jelly roll pan with greased parchment paper
4. Pour pysllium mixture in a large mixing bowl and begin to whisk.
5. Beat in xylitol then lower speed.
6. Add water and vanilla
7. Add flour slowly, do not over mix
8. Pour into pan spreading evenly
9. Place in pan oven and heat to 375
10. Once oven is preheated bake for 12 mins.
11. Cut a sheet of parchment paper or use a dish towel and cover with xylitol.
12. Immediately remove cake and invert on new parchment paper or dish towel.
13. Roll up from the narrow end and allow cake to cool for 30 mins while preparing the jelly
14. Unroll cake and remove paper or towel. Spread cranberry jam evenly on top of cake.
15. Reroll, sprinkle with more xylitol wrap in plastic wrap and refrigerate.

Cranberry Jam recipe:

- 2c cooked cranberries with juice
- 1c xylitol or agave
- ½ water
- 1 ½ T agar flakes

Instructions:

1. Place all ingredients in a medium to large sauce pan and boil over medium heat stirring constantly.
2. Reduce heat and simmer for 10 mins still stirring frequently to prevent burning.
3. Remove from heat and pour in a heat safe bowl to cool.

Chapter 3
Cookies

Chocolate Chip

Ingredients:

- 1c all purpose rice flour blend
- ½ c xylitol
- ½ c brown sugar substitute (date sugar +date syrup)
- 1 stick of Earth Balance shortening
- 2T coconut milk
- 3T water
- 2tsp vanilla extract
- ½ tsp salt
- ½ tsp baking soda
- ½ tsp kuzu+ 1 tsp apple cider vinegar
- 3T coconut flour
- ½ c baker's semisweet chocolate chips

Instructions:

1. Preheat oven to 350, line a cookie sheet with parchment paper
2. In a large mixing bowl combine shortening, xylitol, and brown sugar substitute
3. Add coconut milk and vanilla
4. In a small cup mix kuzu and apple cider vinegar. Add to mixing bowl
5. Add coconut flour salt and baking soda
6. Add water
7. Add flour
8. Fold in chocolate chips
9. Spoon dough into 12 balls, flatten and place on baking sheet
10. Bake for 10-15 mins

Lemon Drop

Ingredients:

- 2 c all purpose rice flour blend
- ½ c xylitol
- 1tsp salt
- 1tsp baking soda
- ½ c palm shortening
- 1T apple cider vinegar
- ¾ c coconut milk
- 1 banana, sliced
- 8T lemon juice
- 4T coconut butter
- 1T Lemon zest+1T xylitol for top (or candied lemon peel)

Instructions:

8. In a small bowl or cup mix coconut milk with apple cider vinegar and set aside (this mixture will look like it is curdling, just let it sit)
9. In a large mixing bowl, blend flour, xylitol, salt, and baking soda.
10. Add shortening, sliced banana, and coconut butter mix until blended into coarse crumbs.
11. Add coconut milk mixture and lemon juice, just stir until mixed do not over stir, the cake will be dense and tough
12. Form dough into a ball, wrap in plastic wrap and refrigerate for 30 mins.
13. Preheat oven to 300
14. Line a cookie sheet with parchment paper.
15. Mix lemon zest and 1T xylitol and put on a plate.
16. Scoop dough into 24 small balls or 12 large balls. Roll out into disk shapes ¼ inch thick
17. Lightly press dough into zest mixture and place on cookie sheet
18. Bake on 300 for 15-18 mins

Orange Spice

Ingredients:

- 2 c all purpose rice flour blend
- ½ c xylitol
- 1tsp salt
- 1tsp baking soda
- ½ c palm shortening
- 1T apple cider vinegar
- ¾ c coconut milk
- 1 banana, sliced
- 8T orange juice
- 4T coconut butter

Topping:
- 1T orange zest +1T palm sugar for top (or candied lemon peel)
- 1tsp pumpkin pie spice (or any combination of ginger, allspice and clove)
- Dash of clove

Instructions:

1. In a small bowl or cup mix coconut milk with apple cider vinegar and set aside (this mixture will look like it is curdling, just let it sit)
2. In a large mixing bowl, blend flour, xylitol, salt, and baking soda.
3. Add shortening, sliced banana, and coconut butter mix until blended into coarse crumbs.
4. Add coconut milk mixture and orange juice, just stir until mixed do not over stir, the cake will be dense and tough
5. Form dough into a ball, wrap in plastic wrap and refrigerate for 30 mins.
6. Preheat oven to 300
7. Line a cookie sheet with parchment paper.
8. Mix orange zest, palm sugar and spices on a plate.

9. Scoop dough into 24 small balls or 12 large balls. Roll out into disk shapes ¼ inch thick
10. Lightly press dough into zest mixture and place on cookie sheet
11. Bake on 300 for 15-18 mins

Cranberry "Oatmeal"

Ingredients:

- 2c all purpose rice flour blend
- ½ c xylitol
- ½ c palm or coconut sugar
- 1c coconut oil
- 4T palm shortening
- 1 plantain, sliced
- 4T raw honey or rice syrup
- 1tsp salt
- 1tsp baking soda
- 2tsp vanilla
- 1 cup dried cranberries

Instructions:

1. Preheat oven to 300
2. In a large mixing bowl, cream together plantain, honey/rice syrup, xylitol, palm sugar, oil, shortening, salt, baking soda, vanilla
3. Slowly add flour 1/3c at a time mix until blended
4. Fold in dried cranberries
5. Line a cookie sheet with parchment paper
6. Scoop cookies into 24 small or 12 large balls, shaped and slightly flatten to ¼ inch thick.
7. Bake for 15-18 minutes

"Sugar"

Ingredients:

- 1c all purpose rice flour
- ½ c xylitol
- 1 stick of earth balance shortening, cubed
- 2T coconut milk
- 2tsp vanilla extract
- 1/2tsp salt
- 1/2tsp baking soda
- 1/2tsp kuzu

Instructions:

1. Preheat oven to 275
2. In a large mixing bowl, cream shortening and xylitol together
3. In a cup mix coconut milk and kuzu, add to shortening mixture
4. Add vanilla
5. Add salt and baking soda
6. Add flour and stir until just blended
7. Like cookie sheet with parchment paper
8. Roll out dough into 12 small or 6 large balls, flatten balls to ¼ inch thickness
9. Put 1T xylitol on a plate and lightly press dough into granules
10. Place cookies on cookie sheet and bake 18-20 minutes
    *options mix a tsp of cinnamon or pumpkin pie spice with 1T xylitol for top, or use palm sugar.

Banana Cream

Ingredients:

- 2 ripe bananas, sliced
- 1c coconut oil
- ½ c xylitol
- 4T palm shortening
- 1tsp salt
- 1tsp baking soda
- 2tsp vanilla
- 3c all purpose rice flour blend

Instructions:

1. In a large mixing bowl, cream together bananas, xylitol, oil, shortening, salt, baking soda, vanilla
2. Slowly add flour 1/3c at a time
3. Cover and refrigerate for 1 hour
4. Cover a surface with ¼ in of rice flour
5. Place dough on floured surface
6. Sprinkle more flour on top of dough and roll out to ¼ inch thick
7. Cut with cookie cutters, (making sure to cut pairs of shapes if you want to make sandwiches) place on baking sheet
8. Bake at 325 for 10 minutes

Cream Filling:
- 2T raw honey
- 4T shortening
- 1/4 tsp soda
- 1/4 tsp salt
- 1/4 tsp xantham
- 1tsp kuzu+2T lemon juice/or apple cider vinegar
- 1 tsp vanilla
- 1/2c arrowroot
- 2T coconut butter

Instructions:
1. Cream honey/agave and shortening together
2. Add coconut butter and blend well
3. Add soda, salt, xanthan and vanilla
4. Separately mix kuzu and lemon juice/apple cider vinegar then add to mixture.
5. Add arrowroot and whip on high until fluffy
6. Once cookies have cooled frost with cream filling and either leave open-face or make sandwiches

Coconut butter

Ingredients:

- ½ c Earth balance shortening
- ½ c coconut butter
- ½ c xylitol
- ½ c palm sugar
- 1 ½ T date syrup
- 1T physillium+1/4 c water
- ½ tsp salt
- ½ tsp baking soda
- 1 tsp vanilla
- 1 ¼ c all purpose rice flour blend

Instructions:

1. In a large mixing bowl cream shortening, coconut butter, xylitol, and coconut sugar until well blended.
2. In a separate cup mix physillium and water until thick, then combine in mixing bowl.
3. Add date syrup and vanilla
4. Then mix in flour making sure to scrape the sides of the bowl. Mix until fluffy and well blended.
5. Cover and refrigerate for 30 mins.
6. Preheat oven to 375
7. Line a cookie sheet with parchment paper, scoop dough into 1 inch balls. Place balls 2 inches apart on tray
8. Slightly flatten the balls with the palm of your hand, then make crisscross lines with a fork
9. Bake for 9 mins, remove from oven and leave on cookie sheet for 10 mins to cool before moving.

Molasses

Ingredients:

- 2c all purpose rice flour
- ½ c xylitol or palm sugar
- 1 stick Earth balance shortening
- 1 ½ tsp salt
- ½ tsp baking soda
- 2 ½ T ginger, either ground or fresh grated
- 1/3 c date syrup
- ½ tsp allspice
- 1/3 c water
- 1 tsp vanilla
- 1-2T xylitol or palm sugar for dusting

Instructions:

1. Preheat oven to 375.
2. In large mixing bowl cream shortening, sugar, salt, baking soda, vanilla, allspice, ginger and date syrup.
3. Add in flour and mix until blended into coarse chunks.
4. Add water and mix until dough resembles playdough.
5. Scoop dough into 1 inch balls, (for crispy cookies freeze for ½ hr before step 5).
6. Slightly roll and press dough between hands to form a disk about 1/4inch thick. Then press dough into extra sugar for dusting.
7. Place on cookie sheet and bake 8-10 mins.

Chapter 4
Muffins

Double Chocolate

Ingredients:

- 1 1/3c all purpose flour
- 4T shortening
- 4T oil
- 1tsp salt
- 1tsp soda
- 1c xylitol
- 4T bean paste
- 4T apple paste
- 3/4c coco powder
- 2tsp vanilla
- 1/2c milk
- 1/2c sparkling mineral water
- 1/2c kombucha
- 1c chocolate chips

Instructions:

8. Cream together shortening, oil, salt, soda, xylitol
9. Add bean paste and apple paste
10. Slowly stir in coco powder
11. Add vanilla
12. Add all liquids
13. Slowly add flour, then whip on high until well blended
14. Add chocolate chips
15. Place in muffin cups and bake at 350 for 25 minutes

Blueberry

Ingredients:

- 2c all purpose flour blend
- 4T bean paste
- 4T fruit fruit puree'
- ½ c sparkling mineral water
- ½ c kombucha
- ½ c coconut milk
- 4Tbsp shortening
- ½ c xylitol
- 1 tsp vanilla
- 1 tsp salt
- 1 tsp baking soda
- 1 ½ c blueberries

Instructions:

1. Pre-heat oven to 350
2. In a large mixing bowl, place shortening, xylitol, salt, and baking soda. Mix until blended.
3. Add in vanilla, bean paste, and fruit puree'
4. Add all liquids
5. Slowly stir in flour until blended then whip on high for 1 min.
6. Fold in 1c to 1 1/2c blueberries
7. Place in muffin cups and bake at 350 for 25 minutes

Banana

Ingredients:
- 1 1/3 c all purpose flour
- 2/3 c coconut flour
- ½ c xylitol
- ½ c palm sugar
- 1 or 2 bananas sliced (start with one and check for desired taste and texture)
- 1T seed mix
- 1/2c coconut milk
- 1/2c kombucha
- 1c mineral water
- 4T palm shortening
- ½ T brown rice syrup
- ½ T date syrup
- ¼ tsp allspice
- 1 tsp salt
- 1tsp baking soda
- 1tsp vanilla

Instructions:
1. Pre-heat oven to 350
2. In a large mixing bowl, mix banana, shortening, xylitol, palm sugar, vanilla, salt, and baking soda until well blended.
3. Add rice syrup, date syrup, and seed mix
4. Add liquids
5. Add flours and mix until well blended
6. Place in muffin cups and bake 25-30 mins

Spice

Ingredients:

- 2c all purpose flour blend
- 4T bean paste
- 4T fruit fruit puree'
- ½ c sparkling mineral water
- ½ c kombucha
- ½ c coconut milk
- 4Tbsp shortening
- ½ c xylitol
- 1 tsp vanilla
- 1 tsp salt
- 1 tsp baking soda
- ½ tsp ginger
- ½ tsp allspice
- Dash of clove
- 1 tsp pumpkin pie spice
- 1T date syrup or maple agave

Instructions:

1. Pre-heat oven to 350
2. In a large mixing bowl, place shortening, xylitol, salt, and baking soda. Mix until blended.
3. Add in vanilla, bean paste, fruit puree', and syrup
4. Add all liquids
5. Slowly stir in flour until blended then whip on high for 1 min.
6. Place in muffin cups and bake 25-30 mins.

Pineapple Upside Down

Ingredients:

- 1 banana mashed
- 1c pineapple chunks
- 1tsp ginger
- 1tsp rice syrup per cup at bottom
- 1tsp salt
- 1tsp baking soda
- 2c all purpose flour
- ½ c sparkling mineral water
- 1/2c coconut milk
- 1/2c kombucha
- 4T shortening
- 1/2c xylitol

Instructions:

1. Preheat oven to 350.
2. Cream shortening, xylitol, salt, baking soda, and ginger
3. Add banana
4. Add liquids
5. Slowly blend in all puropse rice flour. Whip until light and fluffy.
6. Fold in pineapple chunks
7. Fill the bottom of each muffin cup with 1tsp rice syrup then top with muffin batter
8. Bake 350 for 25-30 minutes

Chapter 5
Breakfast

Bagels

Makes 4 servings

Ingredients:
- 2 ¾ c all purpose rice flour
- 1tsp salt
- 2T shortening
- 1T xylitol or palm sugar
- ½ c kombucha
- ½ c sparkling mineral water
- 1 c honey or agave
- 4 quarts water

Instructions:
1. In a large mixing bowl blend flour, salt, and xylitol/palm sugar
2. Cut in shortening until resembles coarse crumbs
3. Add kombucha and mineral water, mix until dough forms into a ball
4. Place ball on counter and cut into 4 equal pieces.
5. Roll pieces out into coils about 4-6 inches long, connect ends of coils to make a circle
6. Place on a tray lined with parchment paper, cover with plastic wrap or a towel and allow to rise 4 hours.
7. Preheat oven to 425
8. In a large pot bring 4 quarts of water and honey/agave to boil.
9. Drop in 2 bagels at a time boil for 1 min on each side
10. Place bagels back on tray and bake for 20 mins

Options: add ½ c dried fruit to dough, top with seeds, dried onions, or spices

Pancakes

Ingredients:

- 2 cups all purpose rice flour
- 3 Tbls xylitol
- 1 tsp sea salt
- 1 tsp baking soda
- 1 Tblsp flax + 2 Tblsp water
- 1Tblsp kuzu+2 Tblsp lemon juice
- 1 c "milk"
- 1 c water
- 2 Tblsp oil

Instructions:

1. Mix flax+water, xylitol, salt, baking soda, oil
2. Seperatly mix kuzu/lemon juice add to bowl
3. Add milk and water
4. Add flour, mix on high until well blended
5. Heat griddle to 300
6. Pour a 1/3-1/2 c of batter for each pancake
7. Wait until air bubbles form on top to flip

Banana Coconut Pancakes

Ingredients:

- 4T oil or shortening
- 1tsp salt
- 1tsp baking soda
- 1/3c coconut flour
- 1 banana mashed
- 1 2/3c all purpose flour
- 1c "milk"
- 1/2c sparkling mineral water
- 1/2c kombucha
- 2T apple cider vinegar

Instructions:

1. Blend oil, salt, baking soda, and banana
2. Add coconut flour
3. Add milk and water
4. Add all purpose flour
5. Add kombucha and apple cider
6. Blend on high until well mixed
7. Heat griddle to 300
8. Pour a 1/3-1/2 c of batter for each pancake
9. Wait until air bubbles form on top to flip

Honey Apple Spice Rolls

Ingredients:

Dough:
- 1 1/2tsp salt
- 1 1/2tsp soda
- 1Tblsp flax+3 Tblsp water
- 2 tsp raw honey, agave syrup, rice syrup
- 3Tblsp shortening
- 3Tblsp oil
- 1/2c kombucha or sparkling mineral water
- 1c "milk"
- 4c all purpose flour
- 1/2c xylitol

Filling:
- 1c palm sugar
- 1c apple paste
- 1T allspice or spices of choice
- 3T honey

Instructions: *Options: top with honey or coconut cream frosting.

1. Preheat oven to 300
2. Mix flax+water, salt, soda
3. Add honey or syrup, shortening, oil
4. Add "milk"
5. Slowly add flour and on high for 10 minutes or by hand for 15 minutes
6. Mix in kombucha or sparkling mineral water
7. Form into ball, wrap in plastic wrap and refrigerate for 1hr
8. In a small bowl, mix filling.
9. Remove dough from refrigerator and roll out to 1/2in thick on a lightly floured surface.
10. Spread a thin layer of filling over the entire surface of the dough. Then begin at one side and gently roll the dough into a log shape.
11. Cut the log into 1in sections. Place sections on baking sheet.
12. Bake on 300 for 15-20 minutes.

Date Rolls

Ingredients:

Dough:
- 2 ¾ c all purpose rice flour
- 1tsp salt
- 2T shortening
- 1T xylitol or palm sugar
- ½ c kombucha
- ½ c sparkling mineral water
- 1/3 c coconut flour for dusting

Filling:
- 1c apple puree'
- 1T allspice
- 20 dates chopped

Instructions:
1. Preheat oven to 300
2. In a large mixing bowl blend flour, salt, and xylitol/palm sugar
3. Cut in shortening until resembles coarse crumbs
4. Add kombucha and mineral water, mix until dough forms into a ball
5. Dust counter surface with coconut flour and roll out dough into an oblong shape about ½ inch think
6. In a small bowl mix filling and spread evenly on dough.
7. Roll dough
8. Wrap dough in parchment paper and bake on 300 for 15-20 minutes
9. Remove from oven allow to cool 5 mins, unwrap roll, completely cool before cutting into slices and topping.

Chapter 6
Pies

Crust #1 (good for pudding & custard pies)

Ingredients:

- 2c all purpose rice flour (option 1 2/3c rice, 1/3c coconut flour)
- 2T bean paste
- 1tsp salt
- 1tsp baking soda
- 7Tbs Earth Balance shortening
- 1 1/2c apple paste (drained puree' or fiber left from juicer)
- 1/2c xylitol or palm sugar
- Parchment paper

Instructions:

1. In a large mixing bowl mix dry ingredients
2. Cut in shortening, apple paste, and bean paste. When well blended form into a ball. If too dry drizzle water, juice or "milk" and continue to mix. Do not add too much liquid.
3. Lay out parchment paper on counter surface. Lightly flour.
4. Cut dough in ½ to make 2 balls.
5. Place one ball one parchment paper, flatten and lightly flour. Roll out into circle shape 1 inch in diameter larger than pie pan.
6. Carefully pick up parchment paper and flip dough into pie pan.
7. Form over lapping edges into pie crust edge by rolling and pinching with fingers.
8. Lightly prick bottom with fork.
9. Either rollout second ball for top crust or use for second pie. *dough may be wrapped and stored in refrigerator.

Crust #2

Ingredients:

- 2c all purpose rice flour
- 8T palm shortening
- Ice water
- Dash of salt

Instructions:

1. Pour flour and salt in a mixing bowl and stir together.
2. Cut in palm shortening until mixed to pea sized balls.
3. Continue cutting motion and add ice water 1T at a time until dough forms a cohesive ball.
4. Cut ball in half and form into 2 new balls.
5. Evenly press 1 ball into a greased pie pan covering the bottom and sides.
6. For top crust roll out second ball on a lightly floured surface and cut into strips or shapes then cover the top of the pie with the pieces.
   *this dough is not elastic like gluten pie dough, it is very difficult to cover a pie with a whole sheet of dough so to prevent breaking cut the top sheet into shapes and then cover the pie.

Custard

Ingredients:

7. 2c juice
8. 3T agar flakes
9. 1c syrup (rice, sorghum, agave)
10. 1/4c raw honey/agave
11. 1 1/4c "milk"
12. 1/4c arrowroot
13. 2 tsp vanilla
14. Pinch of salt
15. Option: 1 vanilla bean scraped, fresh fruit, fruit glaze

Instructions:

1. In sauce pan add juice, agar and salt. Stirring occasionally bring to boil over medium heat. Lower to simmer for 5-10 mins.
2. Add syrup, raw honey/agave and 3/4c "milk" raise heat to medium.
3. In a small bowl, mix 1/2c milk and arrowroot.
4. When the mixture on the stove reaches a boil stir the arrowroot mixture again then add to stove mixture stirring continuously until it becomes thick and bubbly
5. Remove from stove and stir in vanilla.
6. Allow to cool in the pot 10mins then pour into crust or mold. Let the mixture sit 10 more minutes and then pour on topping of your choice.
7. Refrigerate 1hr before serving.

Chocolate Silk

Ingredients: *This recipe makes enough to fill 2 pies

- ❖ 21 squares of unsweetened chocolate
- ❖ 7T shortening
- ❖ 2 3/4c xylitol
- ❖ 10 1/2c "milk"

Instructions:

1. In a double boiler melt chocolate and shortening.
2. Stir in xylitol and heat until dissolved
3. Add "milk" and remove from heat. Whip until mixed thoroughly. Chill. Once chilled whip again until fluffy.
4. Follow pie crust recipe.
5. Bake pie crust on 350 until golden brown.
6. After filling pie crust has chilled, fill shells with whipped chocolate. Refrigerate.
   *Options: top with fruit or "whipped cream"

Apple

Ingredients:

- 8 apples peeled, cored, and sliced
- 1 stick of Earth Balance shortening
- ½ c xylitol
- ½ c brown sugar substitute
- 3 T all purpose rice flour
- ¼ c water
- 1tsp vanilla
- 1 tsp pie spice (any of the following: ginger, clove, nutmeg, allspice, cinnamon)

Instructions:

1. Follow instructions for pie crust recipe
2. Preheat oven to 400
3. In a medium sauce pan melt Earth Balance shortening
4. Stir in flour and mix thoroughly
5. Add water, xylitol, brown sugar substitute and vanilla, bring to a boil over medium heat then reduce to simmer.
6. Arrange apple slices in pie crust, then sprinkle with spices.
7. Place either lattice work top or crumbled top (use dough) on pie; slowly pour hot liquid over pie.
8. Place pie in oven and reduce temperature to 350, bake 35-45 minutes.

Pumpkin

Ingredients:

- 3 ¾ c pumpkin puree', plain
- 1 ¼ c white beans, cooked, rinsed and cooled
- 8 oz coconut butter
- 1 ¼ c palm sugar
- 1 T pumpkin pie spice (or any blend of nutmeg, cloves, allspice, ginger, cinnamon)
- 1 tsp salt.

Instructions:

1. Preheat oven to 375
2. Place all ingredients in a food processor or blender and mix until well blended and creamy.
3. Follow instructions on pie crust recipe
4. Pour filling into crusts and bake for 30 minutes
5. Cool pie and then place in refrigerator to set up before serving.

Whipped cream

Ingredients:

- 1 can whole coconut milk
- 1/3 c xylitol
- 1T arrowroot
- 1T coconut flour
- 1 tsp kuzu
- 1 tsp vanilla

Instructions:

1. Pour coconut milk into a mixing bowl reserving 1T.
2. Whisk in xylitol, vanilla, coconut flour and arrowroot.
3. In a separate cup mix kuzu with reserved coconut milk, then whisk into larger bowl.
4. Pour into container and freeze for 20 mins, then use immediately or move to refrigerator.

Date

Ingredients:

- 1lbs fresh medjool dates
- 1 ¼ c white or red beans, cooked, rinsed and cooled
- 1 apple, peeled, cored and sliced
- 1 tsp vanilla
- ½ c coconut flakes
- Agave syrup to drizzle on top

Instructions:

1. Follow directions for pie crust recipe
2. Preheat oven to 375
3. Place all ingredients, except coconut, in food processor or blender. Mix until well blended resembling pecan pie filling.
4. Pour into pie crusts
5. Top with coconut and drizzle with agave.
6. Bake 30 mins, and cool before serving.

Chapter 7
Scones
All recipes make 6-8 servings

Strawberry

Ingredients:

Scones
- 2c all purpose rice flour blend
- ½ c xylitol
- 1tsp salt
- 1tsp baking soda
- 1 stick Earth Balance shortening, cubed
- ¾ c coconut milk + 1T apple cider vinegar
- 1c chopped strawberries

Glaze
- 1 cup strawberries (chopped)
- ¾ c+2T coconut milk
- 2tsp agar
- 1T agave
- 1T arrowroot

Instructions:

Scones:
1. Preheat oven to 325
2. In a small bowl mix apple cider vinegar and coconut milk, set aside.
3. In a large mixing bowl blend flour, xylitol, salt, and baking soda
4. Blend in cubed shortening until mixture looks like coarse crumbs
5. Add buttermilk and vanilla, do not over mix
6. Quickly add strawberries and stir only until combined
7. Line baking sheet with parchment paper. Scoop batter on to tray use back of spoon or scoop to create and indent in the center of the scone for the glaze.
8. Bake for 18 -20mins.
9. Remove from oven and allow to cool 10mins before adding glaze.

Glaze:
5. In a medium pan add ¾ c coconut milk, strawberries, agar, and agave. Bring to a boil over medium heat.
6. Mix 2T of coconut milk and arrowroot together and whisk into boiling glaze.
7. As soon as the glaze begins to bubble remove from heat and drizzle over scones focusing on the center dip.

Orange Cranberry

Ingredients:

Scones

- 2c all purpose rice flour blend
- ½ c xylitol
- 1tsp salt
- 1tsp baking soda
- 1 stick Earth Balance shortening, cubed
- 1c orange juice
- 1-2T orange zest
- ½ c dried cranberries
- 1T apple cider vinegar

Icing:

Option #1: dairy-free white chocolate chips, melt with 2T coconut milk and drizzle over the top

Option #2:
- ½ c xylitol
- ½ c coconut milk
- 3T coconut butter
- 1T kuzu+2T water
- ¼ tsp vegetable glycerin

Instructions:

Scones:

1. Preheat oven to 325
2. Juice 1-2 oranges, zest entire peels and set aside
3. In a large mixing bowl blend flour, xylitol, salt, and baking soda
4. Blend in cubed shortening until mixture looks like coarse crumbs
5. Add orange juice, apple cider vinegar, and vanilla, do not over mix
6. Quickly add cranberries and stir only until combined
7. Line baking sheet with parchment paper. Scoop batter on to tray.
8. Bake for 18 -20mins.
9. Remove from oven and allow to cool 10mins before adding icing.

*For a strong orange flavor add 1tsp orange extract

Icing:

1. Mix xylitol and coconut milk together pour into small sauce pan with coconut butter. Heat until bubbly, stirring frequently
2. Mix kuzu and water, whisk into pan
3. Whisk glycerin into pan, remove from heat and pour into a heat safe container

Lemon Berry

Ingredients:

Scones:
- 2c all purpose rice flour blend
- ½ c xylitol
- 1tsp salt
- 1tsp baking soda
- 1 stick Earth Balance shortening, cubed
- ½ c lemon juice
- ¼ c coconut milk
- 1-2T lemon zest
- ½ c chopped strawberries
- ½ c blueberries
- 1T apple cider vinegar

Glaze:
- ½ c strawberries (chopped)
- ½ c blueberries
- ¾ c+2T coconut milk
- 2tsp agar
- 1T agave
- 1T arrowroot

Instructions:

Scones
1. Preheat oven to 325
2. Juice 1-2 lemons, zest entire peels and set aside
3. In a large mixing bowl blend flour, xylitol, salt, and baking soda
4. Blend in cubed shortening until mixture looks like coarse crumbs
5. Add lemon juice, apple cider vinegar, and vanilla, do not over mix
6. Quickly add strawberries and blueberries, stir only until combined
10. Line baking sheet with parchment paper. Scoop batter on to tray use back of spoon or scoop to create and indent in the center of the scone for the glaze.
7. Bake for 18 -20mins.
8. Remove from oven and allow to cool 10mins before adding glaze.

Glaze:
1. In a medium pan add ¾ c coconut milk, fruit, agar, and agave. Bring to a boil over medium heat.
2. Mix 2T of coconut milk and arrowroot together and whisk into boiling glaze.
3. As soon as the glaze begins to bubble remove from heat and drizzle over scones focusing on the center dip.

Pumpkin

Ingredients:

- 2c all purpose rice flour blend
- ½ c brown sugar substitute
- 1tsp salt
- 1tsp baking soda
- 1tsp pumpkin pie spice (or ½ tsp ginger, ½ cinnamon or allspice)
- 1 stick Earth Balance shortening, cubed
- ½ c coconut milk
- 1 ½ tsp apple cider vinegar
- ½ c pumpkin puree
- 1tsp vanilla

Instructions:
1. Preheat oven to 325
2. In a small bowl mix apple cider vinegar and coconut milk, set aside.
3. In a large mixing bowl blend flour, brown sugar substitute, salt, baking soda, and spice
4. Blend in cubed shortening until mixture looks like coarse crumbs
5. Add buttermilk and vanilla, do not over mix
6. Quickly add pumpkin and stir only until combined
7. Line baking sheet with parchment paper. Scoop batter on to tray use
8. Bake for 18 -20mins.
9. Remove from heat and sprinkle with extra brown sugar substitute if desired.

Brown "Sugar" & Fig

Ingredients:

- 2c all purpose rice flour blend
- 1 c brown sugar substitute
- 1tsp salt
- 1tsp baking soda
- 1 stick Earth Balance shortening, cubed
- ½ c coconut milk
- 1 ½ tsp apple cider vinegar
- ½ c diced figs
- 1tsp vanilla

Instructions:

1. Preheat oven to 325
2. In a small bowl mix apple cider vinegar and coconut milk, set aside.
3. In a large mixing bowl blend flour, brown sugar substitute, salt, and baking soda
4. Blend in cubed shortening until mixture looks like coarse crumbs
5. Add buttermilk and vanilla, do not over mix
6. Quickly add figs and stir only until combined
7. Line baking sheet with parchment paper. Scoop batter on to tray
8. Bake for 18 -20mins.
9. Remove from heat and sprinkle with extra brown sugar substitute if desired.

References

Date Lady. (2012). Welcome. Retrieved from
http://www.ilovedatelady.com

GetKombucha. (2012). What is kombucha tea?/part 2. Retrieved from http://www.getkombucha.com/what-is-kombucha

Kent, L. T. (2012). What are the benefits of hemp seeds. Retrieved from http://www.livestrong.com/article/167905-what-are-the-benefits-of-hemp-seeds/

Lotus Foods. (2012, c). Organic Madagascar pink rice. Retrieved from http://www.lotusfoods.com/Organic-Madagascar-Pink-Rice/p/LOT-501581@c=LotusFoods@Organic

Lotus Foods. (2012, d). Organic jade pearl rice. Retrieved from http://www.lotusfoods.com/Organic-Jade-Pearl-Rice/p/LOT-00360&c=LotusFoods@Organic

Lotus Foods. (2012,a). Bhutan red rice. Retrieved from http://www.lotusfoods.com/Bhutan-Red-Rice/p/LOT-00160&c=LotusFoods@All

Lotus Foods. (2012,b). Forbidden rice. Retrieved from http://www.lotusfoods.com/Forbidden-Rice/p/LOT-00210&c=LotusFoods@WholeGrain

So Delicious. (n.d.). Why coconuts. Retrieved from http://sodeliciousdairyfree.com/why-coconuts

University of Maryland Medical Center. (2011). Psyllium. Retrieved from http://www.umm.edu/altmed/articles/psyllium-000321.htm

Weil, M.D., A. (2012). Q&A library. Retrieved from http://www.drweil.com/drw/u/QAA365093/Chia-for-Health.html

Wikipedia. (2012, Decemeber 1). Coconut sugar. Retrieved from http://en.wikipedia.org/wiki/Coconut_sugar

Wikipedia. (2012, November 23). Xantham gum. Retrieved from http://en.wikipedia.org/wiki/Xanthan_gum#Allergies

Wikipedia. (2012, November 6). Agar. Retrieved from http://en.wikipedia.org/wiki/Agar#Culinary

webMD. (2012). Flaxseed health benefits. Retrieved from
    http://www.webmd.com/diet/features/benefits-of-flaxseed
wikipedia. (2012, December 4). Xylitol. Retrieved from
    http://en.wikipedia.org/wiki/Xylitol
wikipedia. (2012, February 6). Red rice. Retrieved from
    http://en.wikipedia.org/wiki/Red_rice
wikipedia. (2012, November 12). Arrowroot starch. Retrieved from
    http://en.wikipedia.org//wiki/Arrow
wikipedia. (2012, November 30). Kudzu. Retrieved from
    http://en.wikipedia.org/wiki/Kudzu
wikipedia. (2012, October 28). Black rice. Retrieved from
    http://en.wikipedia.org/wiki/Black_rice

98